Life
Changing
Relationships

Life
Changing
Relationships

Life
Changing
Relationships
BAD BOYS, BAD GIRLS

REVEREND
JAMES T. MEEKS

MOODY PRESS

CHICAGO

Library of Congress Cataloging-in-Publication Data

Meek, James T., 1956-
  Life changing relationships: bad boys, bad girls / James T. Meeks.
    p. cm.
  Includes bibliographical references.
  ISBN 0-8024-2994-7
    1. Mate selection. 2. Mate selection--Religious aspects--Christianity.
3. Man-woman relationshps. 4. Man-woman relationships--Religious aspects--
Christianity. 5. Single women--Psychology. I. Title.

HQ801 .M515 2002
646.7'7--dc21

2001055820

1 3 5 7 9 10 8 6 4 2

Printed in the United States of America

*This book is dedicated to
the members of Salem Baptist Church of Chicago.
These sermons were developed for them
because of their excitement about the gospel
and their love for God's Word.
The members of Salem are the angels
God has loaned me from heaven
who inspire me to study and teach His Word.*

Contents

Introduction

God wants you to experience love beyond your wildest dreams.

Let's be honest with ourselves. Sometimes we question this truth. For many of us, especially women, the years are slowly but surely creeping by. Your friends are getting married, even having children. Perhaps you were in a long-term relationship, had even gotten engaged at one time; the altar was finally in sight, and what happened? The wedding was called off and you were left alone, heartbroken, shattered into a million pieces, wondering whether you would ever find someone, *anyone* to love you.

Maybe you've reached the point where you feel

you're destined to live your life alone. Worn out by the numbers game, you are beginning to realize that you can't cheat Father Time. The Lord is moving you into a new direction, only now you can't define or depend on others to share your vision.

Has it reached the point where you're looking in the mirror asking, *What's wrong with me?* Have you relived every failed relationship you've had since elementary school, scrutinizing every aspect of them as you try to understand what went wrong? Has that person you knew was not "the one" suddenly started looking good to you? Do you find yourself calling your ex-man and/or members of your ex-man's family at all hours of the night, trying to get an explanation of what went wrong in the relationship? Are you on the phone with your girlfriends concocting schemes on how to find a man?

Perhaps you've sunk to an all-time low and have started sleeping with every man that has even thought about looking in your direction or you might be at the other extreme, having sworn that you will never date another man as long as you live because you're tired of all the games—and all of them have a hidden agenda and are up to no good anyway.

As you have looked at past relationships, you might have discovered some destructive patterns in your dealings with members of the opposite sex. You don't want someone who is like your daddy, who essentially was only your momma's roommate, because you never saw any affection or remember seeing them spend any quality time together. Maybe you are attracted to the rebel, the person who will rock your world and show you a side of life you have never seen before. Perhaps you only date married men because you feel they are safe, and you don't want the headache of a commitment.

In your heart, though, you are yearning for love—true love. You've fantasized about your future mate—what he'll look like, his height, his weight—and a good person could be standing right in front of you, and you would not even realize it. Maybe you've just reached the point where you don't know what you want anymore. You don't know if a person is bad for you, so how could you possibly know if one is good for you?

Whether you realize it or not, you are not alone. One of the greatest desires on the earth for both men and women is for companionship. John Donne said, "No man is an island, entire of itself." All of us desire contact and loving relationships with other people, unless you're crazy, like Howard Hughes or some hermit who has decided to live the last twenty-five years alone.

Whether you've never been married or are divorced, don't despair. The time is coming for you to experience love beyond your wildest dreams. Using a few biblical truths, I will show you how to get the kind of relationship you have always desired, how to spot a dog, how to determine whether you are Mrs. Right or Miss Right Now, and how loving others is a direct result of learning to love the Lord.

Now, before I get started, I am going to offer a word

of caution to our brothers. I don't want you-all to think that I'm male bashing or "playa hating" in this book. Quite the opposite. I'm a good man, and I know there are plenty of other good men just like me out there. But in all honesty, many good sisters are overlooking them and running straight to the dogs—those brothers who are up to no good. When it's all said and done, the good men are the ones who have to come in and clean up the mess that some no-good brother has left behind.

I'm directing my message to women, because a great number of them will read this book in hopes of finding out the secrets to obtaining a long-lasting love, and I want to make sure they have the necessary tools.

Rev. James T. Meeks

CHAPTER ONE

The Heat Is On: The Search for Mr. Right

The Heat Is On: The Search for Mr. Right

A s you look around you, it seems that everyone in the world has a mate but you, right? Your momma probably told you when you were little that looks can be deceiving. Just because your best friend has a husband doesn't mean she's happy. You don't know what she is going home to every night. She might be getting beaten up, or maybe her spouse is not even making it home at night. I'm sure that is not the type of relationship you want.

After a certain age, it seems all of us, women especially, have pressure to marry and start a family. Sisters, I am here to tell you, do not listen to that mess that people are talking. Your time will come. Young people, don't worry about not having a date to the prom. It's OK if you are thirty-five and there is no hint of a mate in sight. I tell you that my God is a miracle-working God. He is looking out for your best interests. It's possible that tomorrow the person of your dreams will cross your path. Be about God's business, pray unceasingly, and He will give you the desires of your heart.

You may be thinking that you're not getting any younger, and God needs to get moving soon. Otherwise, you will not have a date for the office Christmas party, in the short term, or you will never have the children you so desire, in the long term. We see things through human eyes. God has a perfect and divine plan. He is more concerned with making sure you have a mate who is pure of heart rather than someone who is the life of the party.

But you want a mate now, you say. It's been five years since you went on your last date. I encourage you to be careful what you wish for, because you just might get it —and regret it. My Christian sisters, I love you–all dearly. I don't want to have to counsel you because someone has given you a sexually transmitted disease. All because you were so busy trying to get a man that you were willing to do anything and everything—including giving him your treasure—to keep him.

Don't allow yourself to start settling for any person that crosses your path. Sure, Pretty Tony looks good, but you and I both know that he doesn't have a job; and brothers, Sexy Shirley's hips might make you take a second look, but she might not know how to spell her own name.

Too often we get caught up in the outer person. Now, there's nothing wrong with wanting someone who looks and smells good, but what about that person's soul? Deep down, you want someone who loves the Lord and who is going to treat you the way you deserve to be treated.

What do you say to those people who are putting pressure on you to find a mate? How do you answer those rumors that have started to spread that you are gay just because it's been so long since you were seen with someone of the opposite sex who wasn't a relative? Tell those nosy people to M.T.O.B. (mind their own business)! God has a plan for your life, and it will be revealed in time.

You have to decide if you are going to listen to God or listen to people. People will give you all kinds of advice about what kind of person you should or should not date. However, they may not have a clue about what they want, or worse yet, they may be putting up with someone just so they can brag to their friends that they have a man. Stick with God's Word and ignore what people are saying to you. Even if it's someone who has your best interests at heart—like your momma or your best friend—don't let them get you down. Look to God, and He will direct your path.

Now before you give up on me because you think that all I'm going to do is preach to you, I'm going to break things down and give you the real deal on how to go about finding a godly mate.

LOOKING FOR LOVE

The story of the creation of humankind is found in Genesis 1:26–27 and Genesis 2:7, 18–24. In Genesis 2:18–22, we find these words: "And the Lord God said, It is not good that the man should be alone; I will make him an help meet for him. And out of the ground the Lord God formed every beast of the field, and every fowl of the air; and brought them unto Adam to see what he would call them: and whatsoever Adam called every living creature, that was the name thereof. And Adam gave names to all cattle, and to the fowl of the air, and to every beast of the field; but for Adam there was not found an help meet for him."

Adam was in the world, and he was alone, but he did not realize that he was alone because he had the animals. As a matter of fact, Adam thought that God was going to find one of the animals to hook him up with. If Adam had had his way, right about now humans could be having dreams about getting married to Miss Piggy or Mr. Ed.

I will never forget this as long as I live. I was preaching to married couples in New Jersey and I was saying, "Brethren, if Adam had made a choice too soon, you could be going home tonight with a bear." One old man sitting on the front row leaned over to another man and said, "He don't know my wife!"

You don't miss what you've never had. This was definitely so in Adam's case. God had to tell the man he needed a wife. God said, "I'm going to make Adam a helpmeet."

Then God paraded all of the animals in front of Adam. Adam looked at them and said, "Are You crazy? I am not marrying a giraffe. I don't care how long her legs are!"

So God made a decision that had a profound effect on humankind. "And the Lord God caused a deep sleep to fall upon Adam, and he slept: and he took one of his ribs, and closed up the flesh . . . thereof; and the rib, which the Lord God had taken from man, made he a woman, and brought her unto the man" (Genesis 2:21–22).

When Adam saw her, he said, "*Now* you're talking!" Or, in the words of the Bible, "This is now bone of my bones, and flesh of my flesh: she shall be called Woman" (v. 23).

You know how woman got her name? When Adam saw Eve for the first time, he looked up to God and said "Whoa, man! That's it! You ain't got to make anything else." Adam was smitten.

It was God who decided that His children should not be alone. When the time was right, He brought Eve to Adam. With this knowledge, you can rest assured that when your time is right, whether it's when you're fifteen or fifty, you will find your mate.

Does this mean that you should sit home alone waiting for your prince (or princess) to come? Absolutely not. Meeting others makes you a well-rounded person. Go to church, join a gym, take part in a book club or investment group. Get yourself in shape, spiritually, mentally, and physically. Sitting home every night isn't going to make your future spouse enter your life any faster. In fact, the time will go by even slower if you just sit there. So get out and live your life, but hold off on the baby until it's God's will that you have one.

ONE IN A MILLION

You might be asking how, in this country of 263 million Americans in general, and 33 million African-Americans, in particular, you will find a mate. Our society has several ways to answer this question. There have been television shows devoted to this topic. Remember *The Dating Game, Blind Date,* or *Who Wants to Marry a Millionaire?* Men and women have gone on national television and answered all sorts of embarrassing questions, thinking that was going to get them a mate. Do you remember any of these couples ending up together? I don't. If you knew a camera was filming everything you did, wouldn't you be on your best behavior? True colors don't actually come out until the camera crew packs up and heads home. That's when you find out that T. William Jones is really Tyrone Jones. You remember him don't you? He was the boy in your fifth-grade class with all the problems. The trouble is, now Tyrone is a grown man, but he is still immature and the problems have not been solved. Guess the camera crews missed that, huh?

We also have computer dating. You connect with someone over the Internet. Now you only communicate with this person via a keyboard. He could be lying about his looks. For all you know, he could be a serial rapist. Don't get me wrong, some people who sign up for computer dating are legitimate. When this is true, it could work out in a positive way, because you actually get to know a person's heart rather than getting caught up in his looks. I'm not saying don't try computer dating—I'm just warning you to be careful.

Then there are the personals. People actually place ads with all kinds of messages—you know, SBF looking for BMW (Single Black Female looking for Black Man Working). But, as with computer dating, there are a lot of crazies out there—plenty of BMWs looking for PYTs (Black Men Walking looking for Pretty Young Thangs) to pay their bills.

Finally, there are singles clubs all across the country. Here in Chicago, we have The Fifty-Yard Line. This place has absolutely nothing to do with football, but it has a lot to do with playing. It's not about the drinking or the dancing. The object of the evening is scoring a bed partner.

DON'T HATE THE PLAYA, HATE THE GAME

Ladies, many of the men you've been dealing with might tell you that I'm "playa hating" because I'm keeping it real. Brothers amuse me with these self-imposed titles. He is "a mack," "a pimp," "a hustler," or a "playa, playa." However, these so-called playas don't have a job, or have a decent credit, or have two teeth close enough together to be called a pair, or have two items in their wardrobe that match. But they have jewelry. Mr. Playa has a watch, eight rings, and some gold chains. Unfortunately, all of them together don't add up to five dollars and fifty cents! Ladies, don't let some broke, no talking, shallow, Mr. T wannabe tell you he's a playa. You need to let Mr. Playa know that if he is a playa, you are the coach; and if he doesn't get his game together, he's going to be benched. Also Mr. Playa, I have a game for you. It's called *be a real man*. First, you get a job; next, you learn to be responsible; and finally, you date one woman and treat her right.

I want the women who name the name of Jesus Christ to meet a high standard. I don't want my Christian sisters to be easy. I don't want you falling for any old line and having sex at the drop of a hat. I tell the women of my congregation that our church is the House of Hope. When brothers come around here, they'd better hope they have the right game. They'd better hope they say the right thing. They'd better hope they live the right kind of life. They'd better hope they have what it takes to get a Christian woman to the altar. If the brother doesn't measure up, leave him on the curb where you found him.

GETTING TO THE GOOD PART

I told you I was going to tell you how to find a mate, and I am a man of my word. Before you begin your search for a man, here are a few things you should know.

1. Don't look for one. The worst thing a person can do who is seeking a mate is to look for one, because if you're looking for a mate, you will always be looking and never trusting in the Lord. And if you're looking at every person you see, you are sizing that person up to see if he has what it takes to be with you.

Adam did not go looking for Eve. God brought Eve to Adam. God knows where you are. He knows where your mate is. You don't have to go looking. You don't have to go to a club every weekend or to the happy hour every Wednesday night. (In fact, you don't need to go to the happy hour at all.) You don't have to look every time the door opens, and you don't have to throw yourself at prospective candidates.

In Proverbs 3:5 we are told, "Trust in the Lord with all thine heart; and lean not unto thine own understanding." Have faith that when the time is right, God is going to lead your mate to you. Why shouldn't you be looking? If you look, you will pick. And if you pick, you are going to pick based on what you see on the outside. You see a guy with wavy hair, but you don't know it's from a kit. Then you go to picking out body parts. "He's got a cute behind." "He's got big hands." "He's got big feet." Can someone please tell me what big hands and big feet mean?

Women devise all these criteria to choose a man. A man with big fingers might have a big bank account, but he might have even bigger debts. As a matter of fact, just because he's got wavy hair and muscles doesn't mean he's not a pervert. He might be a freak. You don't choose anyone based on stuff like how they look. I don't care if he's got big hands and wavy hair. Stop trying to look at a man and size him up.

The Bible says, "The Lord said unto Samuel, Look not on his countenance, or on the height of his stature; . . . for the Lord seeth not as man seeth; for man looketh on the outward appearance, but the Lord looketh on the heart" (1 Samuel 16:7). If you belong to God, let God choose somebody for you. You can only look at the outside. God is looking at the heart. You want somebody with a clean heart. You don't want somebody with big hands. You want somebody with clean hands and a pure heart. Let God pick your mate.

2. Don't give him what he wants. (And men, don't ask for what you want.) Ladies, if you are single and you have hopes of getting married, don't give up your treasure to any man. I don't care how much he begs. I don't care how much he cries. I don't care how much he wants it. I don't care how bad he hurts. I don't care whether he asks you, "What am I supposed to do with this? You mean you're sending me home like this? How am I supposed to sit in the car?" Tell him to put on his coat or go stand outside for a while. (And, by the way, what are you doing to let things get to this state in the first place?)

A brother will come up with all kinds of lines designed to convince you that you must help him out of this predicament that you have put him in. One of my favorites is, "If we don't have sex, I'll explode." Have you ever been walking down a street and seen a man explode? Or, have you ever been to the funeral of an individual whose cause of death was death by explosion? I don't think so.

Ladies, I'm telling you now, brothers will tell you all kinds of stuff. Listen to me: Do not give him what he wants. *Why?* you may ask. Sex with you is not what a man really wants. What he really wants is a woman he can respect. He's really trying to see if you're that kind of woman.

A man will hound you and beg you, but deep in his heart, he's hoping that you keep on saying no, if he's the right kind of man. If he isn't the right kind of man, you don't want him around anyway. You want to weed him out as soon as you possibly can. Trust me, you don't want to waste any heartache, tears, or emotions on a man who does not respect the fact that you do not want to have sex with him.

The other reason he wants you to say no is because he doesn't want to feel that you are that easy. A man knows that if he can have sex with you after one or two dates, he is not the first one to do so. Someone else has been there and done that, too. A man knows that if it was that easy for him to get you into bed, you have been with other brothers before. That knowledge will run him away. The moment you sleep with him, you will run him away. He's thinking, *Yeah, this is a loose woman here.* If he convinced you with his weak rap, talking about, "Baby, I know your feet are tired 'cause you've been running through my mind all day," he knows that you're easy.

Now you can lie and tell him that you've never been with anyone else. You can try to explain that your kids came as a result of you and their daddy just cuddling up. But if he's that dumb, you don't want him anyway.

A man can tell you he loves you, but talk is cheap. Just because he says he loves you doesn't mean he does. Your momma or someone else has probably told you that actions speak louder than words. Believe it! If a man is telling you he loves you, but you live in the same town and only see him once a month, that's a red flag. If you don't have his home phone number and the only time you hear from him is in the wee hours of the morning when he wants to cuddle up, something is not right.

A man who really loves a woman will go out of his way to see her. She will have his home number, his pager number, the number to both his momma's house and his great-aunt Betty's house. He is accessible to her. A man who really wants to be with a woman might not say "I love you" every five minutes, but his actions will show that he cares. He may not be flashy or lavish her with expensive gifts, but he will always be there when she needs him and give her the most priceless gift of all—himself and his time.

The story of Absalom and Tamar is told in 2 Samuel 13:1–20. The first two verses set the scene. "It came to pass after this, that Absalom the son of David had a fair sister, whose name was Tamar; and Amnon the son of David loved her. And Amnon was so vexed, that he fell sick for his sister Tamar; for she was a virgin; and Amnon thought it hard for him to do anything to her."

Tamar was Amnon's half sister, and Amnon couldn't see any way he could have anything to do with her. It would have been "improper," as the *New King James Version* puts it. Yet he was sick with desire for her.

Amnon's friend Jonadab, the son of David's brother Shimeah, saw that Amnon was distressed, and so he asked him, "Why art thou, being the king's son, lean from day to day? Wilt thou not tell me? And Amnon said unto him, I love Tamar, my brother Absalom's sister" (v. 4).

Now Jonadab was a real dog. The Bible says Amnon loved Tamar. And his friend said to him, "Well, man, if you love her, let me tell you what to do to be with her." He didn't offer Amnon a plan for marrying Tamar; he just offered Amnon a plan for having sex with her.

I'm mentioning this to let you know that when you're dating a guy, you should check out his friends, too. As the saying goes, "Birds of a feather flock together." If the guy you have your eye on has friends who are dogs, chances are he's a dog, too. In case you don't know a dog when you see one, we're going to give you some characteristics of dogs to look out for in chapter 2.

Amnon's friend told him, "Man, you're the king's son. Tell the king that you aren't feeling well, and ask the king to send Tamar over to your house. And when you get her there, do to her whatever you want." Is that a dog or what?

So Tamar went to Amnon's house. She "took flour,

and kneaded it, and made cakes in his sight, and did bake the cakes" (v. 8).

Tamar is at Amnon's house now. I'm pointing this out to you because you need to know that you shouldn't be going to any man's house. If you go over to his house, he'll dim the lights and fire up some scented candles. Then he'll start massaging your tired shoulders. Next, he'll take off your shoes and start rubbing your feet. You're already weak because you really are interested in this guy, and now you're trying to deal with his seduction on top of that.

That's why the Bible says, "Make not provision for the flesh" (Romans 13:14). Go out to dinner at a restaurant. That's fine. But be careful about going to a man's house (or letting a man into your house), because once you are there, he is going to make moves on you. It's hard for you to take your shoes off in a restaurant.

When Tamar had baked the cakes, "she took a pan, and poured them out before him; but he refused to eat. And Amnon said, Have out all men from me. And they went out every man from him. And Amnon said unto Tamar, Bring the [cakes] into the chamber, that I may eat of thine hand" (vv. 9–10).

So Tamar brought the cakes "into the chamber to Amnon her brother. And when she had brought them unto him to eat, he took hold of her, and said unto her, Come lie with me, my sister" (vv. 10–11).

You know she probably answered him, "No. Go on, boy. Quit tripping." Seriously, she answered him, "Nay, my brother, do not force me; for no such thing ought be done in Israel: do not thou this folly. And I, whither shall I cause my shame to go? and as for thee, thou shalt be as one of the fools in Israel. Now therefore, I pray thee, speak unto the king; for he will not withhold me from thee" (vv. 12–13).

But Amnon wouldn't listen to her. "Being stronger than she, [he] forced her, and lay with her. Then Amnon hated her exceedingly; so that the hatred wherewith he hated her was greater than the love wherewith he had loved her. And Amnon said unto her, Arise, be gone" (vv. 14–15).

Can you believe that? This man has forced this woman to have sex with him, and then he has the nerve to tell her to get up and be gone. Tamar said, "Man, you ain't gotta treat me like this." But Amnon wouldn't listen. He called his servants and told them, "Put this woman out." He didn't even know her name. Earlier this man was crying about how much he loved Tamar. After he got what he wanted, he didn't even know her name. He called her "this woman."

Now Amnon could win the award for dog of the year, but all the Amnons aren't dead. He's got some cousins, brothers and friends lurking around, and I am trying to save you from them.

There is just something about men, ladies. Once you give up your treasure to a man, he doesn't feel the same way about you as he felt at first. But if you get rid of him prior to having sex, a brother will show up at your job every day when you get off work, rain or shine. He'll be standing there with an umbrella ready to walk you to the train. He will send you flowers every day, write you poetry, and call you every few minutes. But after you have sex, you could get wet or dry up like the wicked witch in the *Wizard of Oz,* and that man will be going on about his business.

Don't give him what he wants. If you want to protect yourself and your reputation, don't give it to him.

3. Check out his definition of love. In today's society, we use the word *love* too casually. Everybody loves everybody. But ladies, you can't love somebody you just met last week. You don't even know him. He could be a serial killer. Don't allow your emotions to dictate to you and control you to the point that everybody you meet you love. How is it possible for you to love somebody you don't know? And not only that, love is one of those things that if you were in love before, the first person you were in love with probably broke your heart. That's the person who taught you what love was all about.

Because you loved that person, you didn't think anything would ever happen. You were expecting to be together forever and to live happily ever after. You gave that man your whole heart, and he took it, squeezed it, and misused it. So you learned from that point on that you don't give all of your heart to just any man.

You cannot give all of your heart to anybody but God, because God is the only one who has the capacity not to break it. You learned that the first time you got your heart broken. Now if your heart has been ripped into a million pieces eight or nine times, that means you are a fool. Everybody plays the fool sometime, but there is no reason for your heart to be broken nine times. That means you have not learned from your past mistakes.

In order to figure out your potential mate's definition of love, *you've* got to have a definition. You can't find out if a man loves you if you don't know what love is yourself.

First Corinthians 13:4–7 says, "Charity suffereth long, and is kind; charity envieth not; charity vaunteth not itself, is not puffed up, doth not behave itself unseemly, seeketh not her own, is not easily provoked, thinketh no evil; rejoiceth not in iniquity, but rejoiceth in the truth; beareth all things, believeth all things, hopeth all things, endureth all things." *Charity* is the old English word for love.

If a man says he loves you, he needs to step up to the plate. We say love suffereth long. Is the person who loves you willing to wait until after you're married to have sex? None of us loves someone who is impatient. If a man really loves you, he isn't going to leave you as soon as he finds out you don't want to have sex. As a matter of fact, you might as well weed out the men who are all about sex up front.

Love is kind. Is the person nice? Love envieth not. A lot of times in relationships, we end up competing. You don't want anybody who is trying to compete with you. Love is not stuck up; love seeketh not his own. Is this person selfish? Love does not anger easily. Watch out for the person who gets mad quickly. Watch out for the person who curses out every car that cuts in front of him. Anybody who gets mad at folks who cut in front of him, people he doesn't even know, he's going to get mad at you just as fast. Love does not get mad fast.

Love does not think bad of you. As soon as your pager goes off, and you have to make a phone call, if the individual is saying, "Who's that? Who are you calling? Where are you going?" that means the person thinks you are like him. He thinks that you are living the kind of life he's living. That's why he doesn't trust you.

Love believeth, beareth, hopeth, endureth all things. Love does not lie. This person you're dealing with, this person you're dating, does not need to take you to some twelve-room house talking about, "This is my house. My auntie and cousin are living with me." By the time you unravel the mystery, you'll find out that the man is broke as a joke, homeless, and all the while he's been living with his auntie and cousin. Be careful, because in relationships, especially dating, lying is a red flag. If a person is lying to you or, you're catching him in lies, don't overlook the lies just because you want the relationship to work. Love does not lie. Isn't it better for him to say, "Hey, I'm living with my auntie and cousin to save some money," than to lie?

Love beareth all things, believeth all things, hopeth all things, and endureth all things. Now if this is your potential mate's definition of love, then you've got something to work with. But if it's not his definition of love, be careful.

Women must understand that men are conquerors. Men are hunters by nature. We like a challenge. We like a goal. Men are not in love with you; they're in love with the chase. Men are goal oriented. If a man is driving from Chicago to Atlanta, all he's thinking about is getting to Atlanta. His heart is fixed. He doesn't care anything about the other people in the car. He doesn't care who has to go to the bathroom or who's hungry. That's not where his head is. He wants to get where he's going, and he's upset if he has to stray from his course.

Anybody who wants to stop had better get ready for an argument. "Why do y'all want to stop? We just stopped six and a half hours ago. What do you think this is? This ain't no trip where you just stop anytime you want. I'm trying to get where we're going. Charlie drove down here last month in fourteen hours, and I know I can beat his time. But not if y'all want to stop every six or seven hours. We ain't gonna be doing that."

When the wife finally convinces her husband that it is important that the children, who are three and four years old, use the bathroom and get something to eat, he'll pull over, but while they're stopped, he's standing around mad. He's looking at the highway, looking at all the cars he passed that are now passing him by. And he's mad that he's lost his truck. He found one of the eighteen-wheelers to follow, and he knew that the truck had a CB and was going fast. And if the truck slowed down, the police were there. Now he has lost his truck because his family made him stop.

When the man finally gets to Atlanta in record time, he's the happiest guy in the car. Everybody else in the car could be dead, but he's happy. He's going to run to the phone and call Charlie and brag. He's going to brag the rest of the trip. Every relative you see he's going to mention how long it took him to get there. That's just a man thing.

The day after Thanksgiving one year, my wife and kids talked me into going to the mall against my better judgment. First of all, the Thanksgiving food was still in the house. My remote control was working. It was warm in the house, and I had a cold. But my family wanted to go to the mall. Everybody knows that the day after Thanksgiving is the biggest shopping day of the year. There were 59 million people in the mall.

So what do I do? I took my family to the mall. You know, love suffers long and is kind, love is patient, love doesn't have to have its own way. But being a man, I'm goal oriented. I wanted to know what we were looking for at the mall.

Here's where men and women are different. Women go to the mall and become one with it. They kind of become connected. Ladies, men aren't really that connected. We're kind of detached from the mall. But my family gave me a goal. We were looking for a black suit for my daughter.

I found nine black suits in one store in nine and a

half minutes. All of them were the size they told me. You know what my family had the nerve to tell me? "OK—well, we're going to see what they've got over there in the other store." That's why they leave me at home. After I had found the suits, I thought we were done.

You send a man to the store with a shopping list with three things on it, and you know how many things he's going to buy? Three. My wife doesn't send me to the store anymore, because when I come home with three things, she gets an attitude, puts her hand on her hip, rolls her eyes and neck—you know, that black woman thing—and says, "You went to the store and all you got was three things? We don't have any butter, eggs, or milk. How could you go to the store and buy only three things?" Then I put my hand on my other hip (I don't want to put my hand on the same hip because I don't want to be at one with her on this hip thing, so I put my hand on the masculine hip), and I start rolling my head and say, "You mean to tell me that we don't have any butter, eggs, or milk, and all you wrote on that list was three things?"

What does all this mean? It means that to a man, a woman is a conquest to conquer. And he'll do anything, and he'll tell you anything to do that. That is why you have to have your own definition of love. Now that you know that a man is goal oriented and a conqueror, don't let him conquer you.

4. Let men know that there is a right way to have you. Tamar looked at Amnon and said, "You don't have to rape me; there is a way to have me. You could ask your father, the king, and he would not withhold anything from you." Ladies, if a man wants to know you better and be in a long-term relationship with you, let him know, "Hey, man, I ain't stuck up, I ain't funny, I ain't hard to please. I've just got a program."

There is absolutely nothing wrong with your having an agenda for yourself. I'm not talking about you trying to manipulate men. I'm saying there is nothing wrong with your knowing what you want. There's nothing wrong with your having a program, and *step one* is, "If you want to be with me, ask the King." That's what Tamar said to Amnon. Ask the king. Ask your father. In other words, tell your potential mate to talk to your heavenly Father about how he should deal with you.

There are two fathers. Your potential mate is either of the devil or he's of God. And if his father isn't your Father, you don't want to hook up with him anyway. There are plenty of married women who will tell you that you don't wait until after you are married to try to get a man saved. You try and get him saved before you get your heart invested in him. You try and make sure that his father is your Father before you get married, because if not, the two of you are going to have different family values.

Step two is, he has got to be able to spend time with you. First, you've got to spend some time with him so that you can find out whether he's cheap. Trust me, you don't want to marry a cheap man. There is no harm in going to a fast-food place, but you don't want to hang out with a man who doesn't know what an upscale restaurant—or for that matter, a *medium* upscale restaurant—is.

You want your potential mate's world to expand a little farther than the corner store. You've got to spend time with him so that you can find out what's in his head. What are his goals and dreams? Does he have a plan for his life?

Next, you've got to spend time with him so that you find out what happened to his last girlfriend. Also, if he's forty-something, you want to make sure he's had a girlfriend before. Anybody who's forty and has never had a girlfriend might have some problems that you might want to be aware of, unless he really has been waiting on God to bring the right person to him. I'm not saying that he definitely *does* have a problem, but time will tell.

As a side note: Don't join in when he's dogging out his ex-girlfriend or ex-wife. You don't know her, and you can't know what she's about. All you know about this woman is what you've heard your man say. Leave her alone. She's not your issue. You don't have anything to do with her.

Get his version of what went wrong with the relationship, and make sure that his past girlfriend is really in the past. You don't want to be a rebound person. If he was married before, spend enough time with him to make sure his divorce is final. You don't want your heart and emotions all tied up only to find out he's still married. Spend enough time with him to make sure he's paying child support. If he's not taking care of his own kids, who are his flesh and blood, he's not going to take care of you, either.

5. Make sure that you come to terms with the fact that you are the marrying kind. Society has tricked you ladies into thinking that there is something wrong with you if you want to get married. If you want a husband, come to grips with the fact that it's OK. You've got to know within yourself that you want a husband, that you are a good woman. Now I'm not saying that when you first meet a man you announce, "You know I want to get married." Make that announcement and you'll run someone away quicker than Superman can fly. Just know within yourself what kind of woman you are. Don't be afraid to say that you are the marrying kind and that you are waiting for your husband to find you. You are waiting for the man that you will spend the rest of your life with. The man who will be the father of your children. You are not looking for a lover. You are not looking to be someone's sex partner.

A man will not buy the cow when he can get the milk for free. Men will try to pretend they don't understand commitment, but they do. Have you ever heard of a family who gets the opportunity to move into a twelve-room house, without a down payment, without paying any rent, without putting down a deposit, and staying there for a year or two to see how they're going to like it? Well, that's what is happening to you women who are living with men you are not married to. Nobody is going to marry you if they're getting all the pleasures and luxuries of marriage without the commitment. A man has no reason to commit to you if you will settle for simply living together.

Let me break it down like this. After you eat Christmas dinner, you do not go back to the store with a bankcard in hand and say, "Hey, y'all, that food I got earlier this week was good, so I want to pay you. I wanted to make sure that my family was going to enjoy it first. Now I'm going to pay for it." You have to make the commitment up front before you get the merchandise. That was my problem with Mr. Whipple. Remember him? Everybody always used to bust him out and say, "Mr. Whipple, please don't squeeze the Charmin." They didn't want him to get it all crumpled. My problem with Mr. Whipple was that he wanted a free feel.

You have to look at a man and say, "Listen, I don't mind getting next to you. I don't mind us getting together, but you ain't gonna squeeze no Charmin in this store. When we hook up and make a commitment, you can squeeze me all night long. As a matter of fact, I'm gonna tell you where to squeeze me. I'm gonna tell you how to squeeze me. But you ain't touching nothing here until we have a relationship."

So ladies, put down the searchlight. Once you acknowledge that you are the marrying kind, you don't have to go looking for a mate. God knows where he is, and He knows where you are. Remember that God's choice for you will not try to get you to give up your "treasure" before the wedding. Also know that Mr. Right's definition of love will be the same as yours. Finally, realize that Mr. Right will come to you in the right way because he is coming with the blessings of your loving heavenly Father.

CHAPTER TWO

Who Let the Dogs Out?

Finally, my brethren, rejoice in the Lord. To write the same things to you, to me indeed is not grievous, but for you it is safe. Beware of dogs, beware of evil workers, beware of the concision.

Phillippians 3:1–2

Who Let the Dogs Out?

Finally, my brethren, rejoice in the Lord. To write the same things to you, to me indeed is not grievous, but for you it is safe. Beware of dogs, beware of evil workers, beware of the concision.

Phillippians 3:1–2

Many women know they want a man, but if you ask them what kind of man, they are clueless. Many are quick to tell you that they don't want a dog or a "playa." Have you really thought about why men are called dogs?

A group called the Baja Men had a popular song out entitled "Who Let the Dogs Out?" To break it down, the song compares the behavior of men to the behavior of dogs. Before we look at men, we need to first look at the behavior of dogs to see if the songwriter has perhaps stumbled onto something.

You know what a dog is, don't you? A dog is a wild animal that has the potential to be tamed and domesticated. However, we have all seen packs of wild dogs roaming around. Their behavior is instinctive; that is, is not learned. They are concerned with finding food, protecting their territory and finding some female to have. Unfortunately, because society and even many parents have given up on our boys, we see groups of them fending for themselves, running around in gangs, protecting their territory and having sex with any and every female they can.

A man is compared to or called a dog, when his behavior resembles that of our four-legged friends.

It makes no difference how a woman thinks, how she acts, how much education she has, how caring she is, or how good she cooks, the number one concern of a dog is the satisfaction of the flesh. If a woman can help him achieve the top item on his agenda, which is the satisfaction of his flesh, then he has time for her. But if she won't cooperate with his plan, since it's not her that he's concerned about in the first place, then the same individual doesn't have time for the lady.

Most women desire something other than a relationship built on the flesh. A woman is looking for companionship. She's looking for friendship. She's looking for loyalty. A woman is looking for a responsible man, someone who is trustworthy, honest, and open. Someone who has morals and integrity.

Ladies, as you look for a man, realize that there are some men who place more emphasis on the flesh than on your feelings, who place more emphasis on their passions than on your personality, who place more emphasis on your hot body than on your heart—you'd better get your leash and mace ready to help you rein in these dogs that have been let loose.

As I said in the first chapter, you must know what kind of man you are looking for. If you allow your passions to control you, and if you don't know the kind of man you want, you are going to fool around and get bitten. Unless you have a program in place to help you discover the kind of man you need in your life, you will have trouble weeding out the dogs from the good men who do exist.

Maybe you have no clue what a "good man" looks like, so how in the world are you going to recognize a man for whom you should *not* be looking? For the sake of discussion, we are going to keep the dog comparison up and tell you some dogs to stay away from.

Just to give you a little background, there are approximately 130 breeds of dog which are broken into seven groups. It would be impossible for me to describe all of them, but I am just going to highlight a few that you should steer clear of at all cost.

THE BULLDOG

The bulldog belongs to the group of non-sporting dogs. They received their name because for more than six hundred years, until it was made illegal in 1835, these dogs were used to bait bulls. The bulldog was also used for dog fighting. This dog is short with a pug nose and wide, powerful jaws. When it sinks its teeth into something, it locks onto it. It is known for its tenaciousness and stubbornness.

Ladies, while you're searching for a mate, watch out for the bulldog. You will recognize him because he's the man who always has to have his way. When you run up on this brother in an argument, he will stay in the argument just so he can prove you wrong. Beware of a man who can never give in. Beware of a man who can never go along with you on issues. Steer clear of a man who is always angry. Every time you see him, he looks like he's been chewing nails.

I've got a secret for you: If you can't handle this kind of man while you are dating him, you might as well hang it up, because you surely are not going to handle him after you get married. This man—or this type of dog, if you will—does not become milder. If anything, he will become more and more stubborn after the wedding vows.

I want you to know that you are better able to persuade the guy you are dealing with while you are single than you will ever have after you're married. If you can't deal with him while he's single, you need to leave the bulldog where he is.

THE CHIHUAHUA

The Chihuahua is the smallest breed of dog. It is six to nine inches high and weighs anywhere from two to six pounds. That is as large as a Chihuahua will ever get. The Chihuahua is in the group known as toy dogs.

My sisters in Christ, be careful of the Chihuahua. These are the men who will never grow up. They are in the Peter Pan Syndrome. Be careful because some of you are dating Chihuahuas right now. You don't want to take this man to the altar because Chihuahuas don't want to accept responsibility. Chihuahuas don't want to be men.

You see, it's all right to play basketball. There is nothing wrong with playing baseball, and playing video games on occasion is no big deal. But there is something wrong with a grown man who carries around a GameBoy Advance or has a Sega Genesis or PlayStation 2 in his bedroom. Something is wrong with a man who watches Nickelodeon or the Cartoon Network all day long and doesn't have a job. I warn you, ladies, to be careful.

"Well, Pastor," you might say, "how will I know if I've got a Chihuahua, because the man I'm dating is six feet five?"

A Chihuahua is a man who can't hold a decent conversation. He can't hold his head up and look you in the eye when he's talking to you. A Chihuahua is a man who won't talk about current affairs. He thinks that mess with O. J. Simpson is current news. A Chihuahua is a man who doesn't watch the news or read the newspaper. How can you live in this day and age and not watch the news, read the newspaper, or know what's going on in the world? If the only thing your man knows is the score of last night's football game or when his favorite rap artist's new

CD or the latest Jordans will hit the stores, that is a major problem.

Now I want you to know—and I realize this may seem petty and might push some buttons—but if his momma didn't raise your man, what makes you think you can? Don't waste your time. He was a little boy when you found him, he was a little boy when he got to you, and right now he is just a little boy with a mustache, beard, and some grown-up clothes. The Bible says in 1 Corinthians 13:11, "When I was a child, I spake as a child, I understood as a child, I thought as a child: but when I became a man, I put away childish things." If your man has not put away childish things, then leave him and move on.

THE GERMAN POINTER

Most of us know about German shepherds, but let me tell you about the German pointer. This type of dog is good for bird hunting because once the bird is shot out of the sky, the German pointer points toward the bird to direct the hunter.

Watch out for the man who is a pointer. Be careful of the man who points to somebody else as the reason for his not advancing out of a dead-end job. Watch out for the man who points to the white man as the reason he doesn't have a job. Now it doesn't matter that he hasn't gone out to look for one. He thinks he's too good to work at McDonald's because it doesn't pay enough. He can't work in the mailroom because it's too demeaning. He won't work for a moving company because he doesn't want to lift anything heavy. He won't deliver papers because he has to get up too early in the morning. He can't work nights and weekends because he wants to hang with his boys.

Ladies, trust me, this is not the kind of man you want to be with. You want someone who is going to provide for you to the best of his abilities. If taking care of his family means getting up at three every morning and picking up cow manure, then a real man will do what he has to do to make sure his wife and children have food on the table and clothes on their backs.

Ladies, stop turning up your noses at men you feel are beneath you because of the kind of work they do for a living or because they didn't go to college. Many of you have these grandiose dreams of marrying a doctor, lawyer, or some man with a spectacular job. Or you're looking for a man with all these degrees, but you forget that you barely graduated from college yourself.

Having a college degree is a fine thing, but there are a lot of educated fools running around. Which is better, having a man who drives a bus or delivers the mail who will work, or having a man who will not work because he can't find a job in his field? It's not about eating steak every night or wearing the latest designer fashions. You want someone who is going to be there for you when times get tough. You want someone who is going to make you laugh, and who has your best interests at heart. You want a man who is going to take care of his children. Don't get hung up on this man that you dreamed about when you wre a little girl. You're an adult now. Adults should know how to compromise when it is appropriate and right. They should know the difference between dreams and reality.

Now, I won't deny that blacks, especially men, have suffered injustices in this society, but white men don't have anything to do with a grown man not getting up and going out to look for a job. There is no one holding you down in bed every morning telling you not to go out and fill out job applications. Ladies, you don't need a man who is telling you that rather than work at McDonald's, he is going to sit home and let you take care of him and not contribute anything to his household.

Your man is no man if he's letting you take care of him, and you come home to a nasty house, kids running around filthy, and no food on the table because cooking and taking care of the house and kids is "women's work." You are not much of a woman if you are allowing someone to take advantage of you this way. I'm not trying to hurt any feelings, but if you want to know how to have a life-changing relationship, I am just going to keep things real.

Watch out for the man who points to the preacher as the reason why he doesn't go to church, giving those tired excuses, "When I was a little boy, my momma had the preacher over and the preacher ate up all the chicken." Well, you're a grown man now, so what's your excuse?

Watch out for the man who blames everyone but himself for the shape he's in. "Well my momma and them, they favored my brother over me. And when I was a little boy, my brother got his own room, but I had to sleep in the room with my cousin." Well, you are a grown man now. Why are you still sleeping in the room with your cousin at twenty-seven? At thirty-six, why are you still sleeping in a room in your momma's house? That isn't your momma's fault. It might have been her fault when you were ten, but not when you are forty.

Watch out for the pointer, because he will always blame his boss. "That's why I ain't got a job, 'cause of my boss or because of society." Whenever you find a man who says his situation is always someone else's fault, get away from him. Run. Do not pass go! Do not collect $200! A man—a real man—takes responsibility for his actions. A real man will stand up and be accountable. A real man will not point to others and blame them for being the cause of all his troubles.

THE BOXER

As I continued my research, I discovered another dog I need to mention. The boxer, like the bulldog, is used for police work. Boxers make good watchdogs, and they are great bodyguards. You know why? Because they are fighters. Watch out for the man who likes to fight.

Ladies, before I go further, let me tell you what I don't get. Maybe someone can e-mail or fax me and help me to understand this. Why is it that a woman will marry a man who beat her while they were going together? Does she thinks the marriage vows will cause a transformation, and Boxing Bruce, who has sent her to the hospital six times, will suddenly give up his violemt behavior? For the life of me, I can't figure it out. Somebody's going to have to help me on this one. What would motivate you to marry a man who beats you up while you are going together?

And for those of you who think your man loves you because he hits you, you're crazy. It's just that simple. You have got to be a fool if the way you spell love is B-E-A-T upside your head. I encourage anyone who is reading this, who is married to or dating a boxer, to get your boxer—and yourself—some help.

God does not want you to be with a man who abuses you. If a man cannot treat you as a queen, if he cannot treat you like delicate merchandise, if he cannot treat you better than he treats his car (he washes his car; he shines his car; he polishes his car; he paints, deodorizes, and re-freshes his car), he is not the person you should be with. Somebody slams the door of his car and he says, "Hey, don't be slamming the door of my car!" Anybody who has a problem with you slamming the door of his car, yet he doesn't have a problem slapping you upside the head, why are you going to marry him?

Stay away from the boxer. Boxers need help. Boxers need counseling. Boxers need to go see a doctor. And if you're with one, so do you.

THE GREAT DANE

The Great Danes is a big pretty old dog. It is a graceful animal that makes a fine watchdog. But primarily, the Great Dane is an excellent companion dog. As we continue the analogy between the behavior of some brothers and various breeds of dogs, what I'm trying to tell you is to watch out ladies, for Pretty Tony. Be careful, because Pretty Tony is out there. He might even be sitting next to you while you're reading this book.

Pretty Tony is good-looking. Pretty Tony is a sharp dresser. Everything that Pretty Tony has on matches. If he's wearing gym shoes, they have the same colors as his jogging suit. Even his baseball cap matches the shoes and the jogging suit. Pretty Tony's fingernails are manicured. Now there is nothing wrong with what I have just described. You want your man to look and smell good, but Pretty Tony's problem is that he wants you to pay for everything. Pretty Tony wants you to get his nails done. He wants you to get his clothes out of the layaway. Pretty Tony wants to use your credit card, because he doesn't have any credit. Pretty Tony wants a car, but he wants you to cosign for it.

Shame on you if you are cosigning for some man's car because he can't afford to pay for his own. You might tell yourself and others, "I was just trying to help him get back on his feet." No, you weren't trying to help him out; you were trying to buy a man. Ladies, don't buy a man, don't rent a man, don't borrow somebody else's man.

Wait on God to give you your own man. You don't have to buy a man. You are a child of the King. You are a daughter of God. God doesn't want you to rent, buy, or share a man.

So ladies, even though Pretty Tony looks good on your arm, and everybody says, "Whoo, child, who is that? He is fine. He is da bomb," be careful! Pretty Tony can rap. He can tell you stuff that will make your head spin. But don't forget that Pretty Tony will tell you what you want to hear because he needs his coat out of layaway.

THE IRISH SETTER

The Irish setter, which is also a sporting dog, behaves differently from the German pointer. This breed fascinates me. The Irish setter also works with the hunter. When a bird is shot down or wounded, the Irish setter smells the air to locate the bird. It runs to where the bird is and just sits. That's why he's called a setter. He just sits right there waiting until the bird dies or until his master comes.

There are some men who, when they see a wounded woman, will come find you and just sit. There are men out there who will take advantage of your inner emotional state. What they are looking for? If you'll allow me to break it down, they are looking for a woman on the rebound.

Irish setters are the brothers who will find a woman who has been hurt, who has been wounded, so they can comfort her. They'll feed you when you're hungry and comfort you when you're lonely. They will help you dog out your ex-boyfriend. They will look at you and say, "How could anybody walk away from a woman like you? How could anybody hurt somebody as sweet as you? Why, if you belonged to me, I'd never let a tear fall from your eye. As soon as I saw a tear about to roll down your cheek, I'd say, 'You bet' not! 'Cause this jewel belongs to me.'"

When you find an Irish setter in church, he wants to become your prayer partner. He wants to call you in the morning so the two of you can read the Scriptures and pray about this dilemma you're going through. Watch out now! When you're wounded, when you're hurt, when you're coming out of a bad relationship, that's the worst time to get involved with any man on any level. That's the time to be quiet. That's the time to be still and know that He is God (Psalm 46:10). That's the time for questions and stillness (Isaiah 30:15). That's the time to figure out what God is saying to you. It is not the time to let some sly, fast-talking man come around and just sit alongside your wounded self.

THE COCKER SPANIEL

Ladies, you need to buckle your seat belts, because I hear the engines revving up. I know the roof is about to blow when I tell you watch out for the cocker spaniel! I don't have to tell you what he's after, do I? For him, all roads lead to the same thing, be it your house or his car.

The cocker spaniel doesn't talk, he doesn't want to get to know you, he doesn't want to establish a relationship, he doesn't want a friendship. You don't matter to him at all. The cocker spaniel is all about sex.

Watch out for the person who, after he finds out you can't do anything for him, doesn't want to talk to you at all. Ladies, this is why you have to be up front what you are or are not about. You have to establish in the beginning what you're going to do and what you're not going to do. You've got to keep it real: "This is who I am, and here are my boundaries. I don't mind going to the show with you, but just because you take me to the show, you ain't gonna go to no bed with me. If that is the price I have to pay, I can pay for the show myself. I can drive myself and meet you there. And shame on you, if you think I'd give it up for a $7.50 show ticket!"

And ladies, shame on you if you can be had for the price of a movie ticket and an extra-value meal from a fast-food place. Shame on you, if you're only a Quarter Pounder deep!

THE HOUND DOG

The breeds of dogs that belong to the group known as hound dogs are great hunters. They are used by police to find missing persons and escaped criminals. The hound dog we are most familiar with is the big ol' wrinkled-looking bloodhound. Whenever we see this dog, it is in a movie, he is just lying around, so we associate this dog with laziness.

Watch out for the man who won't fix himself up, whose hair is unkempt and whose clothes are wrinkled. These could be signs of a deeper problem. But maybe the brother just doesn't think that it takes all that. He's working and that's enough.

Well, if you have to choose between Pretty Tony, who looks and dresses nicely but you have to pay for it, and the hound dog, choose the hound dog because he's wrinkled but he's working.

★ ★ ★

Ladies, please know that I'm not saying that all men are dogs. Dogs were the first animals to be tamed and domesticated and they have proved to be very helpful to mankind. They are said to be man's best friend. Or woman's best friend, as the case may be. But the dogs *are* out there!

The Bible says that everybody who puts emphasis on the flesh and denies the Spirit is a dog. When you see him, a dog by any other name—might be Barry Bulldog, Charlie Chihuahua, Percy Pointer, Bruce Boxer, Pretty Tony, Sidney Setter, Sly Spaniel or Howard Hound Dog—he is still a dog. A child of God does not go to the kennel or the pound looking for a man.

Could This Be You?
Are You Mrs. Right
or Miss Right Now?

CHAPTER THREE

Could This Be You?
Are You Mrs. Right
or Miss Right Now?

I've taken the men through the wringer and raked them over the coals. Now it's time for you ladies to be placed on the hot seat. Many of you say there are no good men available, but I'm sure if you search your heart, you'll realize that's not true. There are plenty of good men. Your daddy was probably a good man. Your granddaddy probably still rates number one in your book, and your brothers might get on your nerves, but deep down, you know they have your best interests at heart. What makes these men good? What characteristics do they possess? If you look around, you'll discover other men with these qualities.

Maybe the problem is you. Is there a possibility that

all the good men are passing you by because you are not a good woman? Singer Donna Summers had a song out a long time ago touting the attributes of bad girls. Women across the country were dancing in the streets celebrating these women. Maybe you were one of the bad girls, and this became your anthem. Perhaps you didn't realize you were a bad girl then, but now, in hindsight, you realize that you were out there. You are not the same woman now that you were then, but you still desire a relationship with a man.

You might be at the point now where you see all of these women getting attention from men, and you're wondering if your standards are too high. You're thinking maybe you need to loosen up a little, let your hair down, so to speak. I warn you to stay true to yourself. Watch out the kind of women you hang with so that you are not guilty by association.

In the book of Proverbs, Solomon asked a straightforward question. He didn't bat an eye; he didn't beat around the bush. He simply asked: "Who can find a virtuous woman?" (Proverbs 31:10). The word *virtue* means morally pure, or good. In other words, Solomon was asking, "Who can find a good girl?" And then he added, "For her price is far above rubies. The heart of her husband doth safely trust in her, so that he shall have no need of spoil" (vv. 10–11).

A good woman is rare. If she could be found, she would be priceless. Anything that is common, that can be found in bunches, is a dime a dozen. But something that you can't find on every corner is priceless. A good girl is unique.

Solomon was not a dumb guy. First of all, he was probably "the man" when it came to women. He had a thousand of them—seven hundred concubines and three hundred wives (1 Kings 11:3). We also know he was not a dummy, because the Bible says that Solomon was the wisest man who ever lived (1 Kings 3:12). And yet even he found that one of the most difficult things to do in all the world was to find a good girl.

If good girls were hard to find three thousand years ago when Solomon was looking, think how hard they are to find today. Solomon was looking before television, before MTV, before Madonna suggested that material girls should live in a material world, before birth-control pills and before women's liberation. Today the search would be like trying to find a needle in a haystack.

Some of you ladies might beg to differ, but I am afraid that women's liberation, along with the feminist movement, has caused women to desire to compete with men. Now don't get me wrong. I bet right now some of you ladies are getting an attitude because of what I've just said. I can see you now, rolling your eyes, your neck going where no man has gone before, but ladies, I'm just keeping it real.

I honestly believe that women should receive equal pay if they are doing the same job. If a woman is qualified and able to pass the same tests a man does, she should be a police office or she should be able to work in the

fire department. Women should be able to run for pub-
lic office or manage an office. Nothing is wrong with a
woman competing with a man in the employment arena.
But the competition should not consist of who is going
to have the lowest morals.

Regardless of how low men sank, it has always been
commonly thought that women would have greater respect for themselves. A man might choose to sleep with
everything that's walking, but men have always thought,
we've always hoped, we've always believed, that women
would have a higher standard. What's next, are you going to put a mark on your bedpost for every guy you've
slept with?

Ladies, you cannot compete with a man on who can
sink to the lowest level. Why would you want to compete
on who is going to scrape the dirt out of the bottom of
the gutter? You have got to be about much more than
that, and you have got to have more respect for yourself.
You are a daughter of God! You've got to have more faith
and trust in God and respect for yourself.

I believe it is difficult to find a virtuous woman or a
good girl because good girls are being influenced by bad
girls. I know that from the outside looking in, it appears
as though the bad girls are having more fun. Bad girls
paint a picture of their lives and it seems like they've got
it going on, like they have everything together.

You see them on college campuses. You see them out
in the street. There always seems to be a crowd of people around them, yet the good girls are by themselves.

Ladies, especially my good girls, I want you to know that there is a reason the crowd is around the bad girl. Bad girls are crowd pleasers.

Ladies, it is better to be by yourself with your self-respect intact than to have your name and number plastered on the bathroom walls. It is better to be able to hold your head up than to be the talk of the office because of your low moral standards. But enough of my preaching. Let me give you five characteristics of bad girls. I know I'm going to step on a few toes, but bear with me.

TALKING 'BOUT BAD GIRLS

1. Bad girls ask men for sex. The story of Joseph and Potiphar's wife is given in Genesis 39:1–20. Verse 7 sets the scene: "It came to pass after these things, that his master's wife cast her eyes upon Joseph; and she said, Lie with me." Potiphar's wife wanted to have relations with Joseph. She didn't hide it; she didn't beat around the bush. She went for the direct approach. She said, "Joseph, let's get it on."

But Joseph refused to do this. "Behold, my master wotteth not what is with me in the house, and he hath committed all that he hath to my hand; there is none greater in this house than I; neither hath he kept back anything from me but thee, because thou art his wife: how then can I do this great wickedness, and sin against God?" (vv. 8–9).

But Potiphar's wife was persistent, and she was hoping that her persistence would wear Joseph down. Day after day she asked Joseph to sleep with her, and day after day he refused. Then one day when Joseph went into the house to do his work "there was none of the men of the house there within. And she caught him by his garment, saying, Lie with me: and he left his garment in her hand, and fled, and got him out" (v. 11–12). When Joseph fled, he left in such haste that he didn't even try to take his cloak with him. Potiphar's wife took this garment and used it to lie to her servants, telling them he had tried to attack her and had left it behind when she cried out. Potiphar was furious and ordered Joseph thrown in jail.

Many women today are like Potiphar's wife. I know it sounds like a fairy tale, but once upon a time, women played hard to get. There used to be a time when women waited for men to be attracted to them. But nowadays, bad girls don't wait to be pursued, they become the chasers.

When I was growing up, we used to play a game called Catch a Girl, Kiss a Girl. The object of the game was for the boys to chase a girl down and kiss her. Now, the girls in my neighborhood were all related to the track stars Florence Griffith Joyner and Jackie Joyner Kersee. All the girls in my neighborhood could have been Olympic track stars. You'd see them, they'd be running, and you didn't hear anything but wind blowing and arms flapping. All of the girls from my neighborhood in Englewood could have gone to Sydney, Australia, and won every Olympic running event. All of them were fast—and I'm talking about their running skills.

There was always one ol' fast-acting, nasty girl who would fall down. And she'd lie there on the ground talking about, "I'm hurt. I think my leg is broken. Somebody come help me." Everybody would be running past her, and she'd say, "Hey, y'all, don't you know the rules of the game?" She'd be reaching up, grabbing boys, trying to trip them and stuff in an effort to get her kiss.

Ladies, again you must have self-respect and love yourself more than that. As a matter of fact, a lady would rather wither up and die or have pimples on her face the size of a dime, than to lower herself by asking a man to go to bed with her. You are *somebody*. You are a King's kid. You are royalty. You are not the pursuer. You are to be pursued. If you ask somebody for sex, I am telling you now that you are a bad girl, and you are not respecting yourself.

Women today say, "I know what I want and I go after it. I'm not shy. I'm not going to be a Wanda Wallflower standing around waiting for somebody to say something to me." That's not what the man you're trying to get with hears when you say that. What he hears is "This is somebody who is hard up, who can't get a man, who couldn't wait for a man to come to her."

You may see yourself as this tough, independent woman who knows what she wants, but what he sees is someone who is easy and desperate. That's where dogs like Pretty Tony come in. Sisters, I am warning you, you are in for lots of heartaches and problems if you don't sit yourself down and wait for God to send you somebody.

Let me tell you something: Married women are not asking their husbands for sex. I teach marriage conferences all across the country, and married women relate a similar tale of the time, fifteen years ago, they put on a sexy nightgown, splashed on some Chanel No. 5 perfume, lit some candles, and had some Luther Vandross playing softly in the background only to have their husbands not respond. So they don't ask anymore. Married women are the only ones who *can* and *should* be pursuing their men. Here's the paradox: Married women are the only ones who should be asking for sex from their husbands, but they aren't. And single women shouldn't be asking for sex, but they are.

2. Bad girls get pregnant on purpose. The Bible says that Lot's daughters were afraid that their seed would pass away, that is their family line would vanish, and so they decided to sleep with their daddy in order to get pregnant.

You don't believe me? Read Genesis 19:32–36: "Come, let us make our father drink wine, and we will lie with him, that we may preserve seed of our father. And they made their father drink wine that night: and the first-born went in, and lay with her father; and he perceived not when she lay down, nor when she arose. And . . . on the morrow, . . . the younger arose, and lay with him. . . . Thus were both the daughters of Lot with child by their father."

Sex outside of marriage is wrong! Ladies, I won't lie

to you. Sex feels good. In fact, sex is good because it was made by God. But it was made for the marriage bed. It doesn't matter that this is the man you are going to spend the rest of your life with. Until you have that ring on your finger and the marriage license is signed, sealed, and delivered, sex is a no-no. (Before you ask, oral sex is included.) Leave it *all* alone until after you say, "I do."

Shame on you if you get pregnant because you think that the pregnancy will increase your chances of getting married. You are living in the wrong day and age. Back in the old days, a man would do the honorable thing and marry you if you got pregnant. But now, if a man doesn't love you, if he doesn't care about you, and if he doesn't want you, he will leave you and the baby right where you are and go on about his business. He will marry a good girl and not think twice about you.

Ladies, you should want a man to love you because he loves you. You should want to be with a man because he adores you. You should want to be with a man because he cares about you and can't live without you. You should love a man because he says, "The last thing I think about before I fall asleep is you. The thing that I think about in the middle of the night is you. The first thing I think about when my feet hit the floor is you. As a matter of fact, heaven must be missing an angel because you're here with me right now. Heaven must have sent you from above. Heaven must have sent your precious love." You've got to want a man because he wants you, not because you've figured out how to trap him with a baby.

And shame on you when you get older, and you've got to have a baby because your clock is ticking. It doesn't matter if you say, "Me and my baby's daddy agreed that he was going to get me pregnant, and it was going to be my responsibility to raise the baby." It's still wrong.

3. Bad girls sleep with men for money. Judges 16:4–5 reads, "It came to pass afterward, that [Samson] loved a woman in the valley of Sorek, whose name was Delilah. And the lords of the Philistines came up unto her, and said unto her, Entice him, and see wherein his great strength lieth, and by what means we may prevail against him, that we may bind him to afflict him: and we will give thee every one of us eleven hundred pieces of silver."

When we tell the story of Samson and Delilah, a few details are left out. One is the fact that Samson really loved Delilah. As a matter of fact, that's how Samson got Delilah, because he loved her so much. His love for her was so great that he told her a secret he promised God he wasn't going to tell anybody.

Samson loved Delilah, but Delilah was looking to get paid. She wanted some money, and the Philistine lords promised that each of them would pay her eleven hundred pieces of silver. Now eleven hundred of anything is a lot, even if it's only eleven hundred pennies. Can you imagine a bunch of people telling you that they were each willing to pay you eleven hundred pieces of silver? Delilah slept with Samson because she wanted some money.

A bad girl will find a man who doesn't mind giving

her money. She will hook up with a sugar daddy. And you know that sugar daddy is usually some old man, with gold chains around his neck and a whole bunch of rings on his fingers, who wants to be near a woman so badly that he's willing to empty his bank account just so that he can go around his friends and brag about what he's doing, when you know he really ain't doing nothing.

Bad girls find themselves a sugar daddy, somebody they think can supply them with things. Bad girls see a coat they want, they see shoes they want, they see some jewelry—and they make a call or trip to Mr. Sugar Daddy. Don't let a sugar daddy start talking about taking them on a vacation. . . . A sugar daddy tells her he's going to take her to Gary, Indiana, and she gets all excited. And don't let him mention Hawaii. Don't let him mention anyplace where there is some sand, beach and some water. A bad girl who wants clothes or vacations is what I like to call your "special-item bad girl." She has some special item in mind, so she's going to sleep with a man to get it.

You also have your "utilities bad girl." Rent. Car note. Light bill. Phone bill. She will sleep with a man to get her bills paid. Ladies, I want to let you know that anybody who sleeps with a man for money, whether you want to admit it or not, is a prostitute. Don't go to rolling your eyes and snaking your neck again. You *are* a prostitute!

Now, I've got three daughters. How would it reflect on me as a father if one of my daughters had a sugar daddy? If my daughter is sleeping with somebody for a watch, a ring, or rent money, I didn't do something right when I was raising her. It would make me look as a bad daddy because my daughter would be sleeping with some man for money.

You might say, "My daddy is dead." Or, "He's alive and he don't care." No, he's not. You said you are saved. You said you have been born again. Well, your Father is rich in houses and land. He holds the wealth of the world in His hands. Sleeping with men for money makes God look bad. How is it that you, a child of God, think you've got to sleep with somebody in order to get your bills paid? Before you dishonor God in that way, it would be better for you to live in your momma's basement, or to live in a one-room shack, or to have your own little place than to sleep with some man and live on the ninety-ninth floor of some luxury apartment building and be a prostitute.

It is better for you to take the coat that you wore last year, sew the ripped seam, patch the hole in the pocket, put it on and hold your head high than to have a mink coat and be a prostitute. It is better for you to get your old car tuned, buy some new tires, and get a new paint job, than to have a new car and be a prostitute.

You might say, "I deserve the finer things in life." I'm not saying you don't. Get a real job. Go to work. Pay your own way. You don't have to resort to sleeping with men for money to get what you think is your just due.

God does not require you to sleep with men for money. That is not what He means when He says He will supply all of your needs.

Now you're probably thinking I'm not talking to you.

You might think I'm talking to your little sister, your cousin, your auntie, or your momma. Mothers will tell you, "Girl, you're out here struggling. You'd better get somebody to take care of you." Don't reduce yourself to the level of sleeping with a man because you need somebody to take care of you.

4. Bad girls use their bodies to manipulate men.
Mark 6:21–24 tells us that "when a convenient day was come, . . . Herod on his birthday made a supper to his lords, high captains, and [the] chief [officials] of Galilee; and when the daughter of . . . Herodias came in, and danced, and pleased Herod and them that sat with him, the king . . . sware unto her, Whatsoever thou shalt ask of me, I will give it thee, unto the half of my kingdom. And she went forth, and said unto her mother, What shall I ask? And she said, The head of John the Baptist."

The Bible says Herod had a party. He and a bunch of other old men where sitting around getting drunk, and a young girl, Herodias's daughter, started dancing. She danced so well Herod said to her, "Ask of me whatever you will, and I will give it to you, even to the half of my kingdom." The girl went and asked her momma, "What should I ask for?" Her momma said, "Ask him for the head of John the Baptist."

This was a bad girl using her body to manipulate a man.

Now, ladies, you know all the men on your job are looking at you. That's why you wear all those tight fitting clothes. That's why you unbutton that button on

75

your blouse and wear the slit in your skirt so high. You know that the men are looking at you. Men are excited by what they see, and if they see the right thing, they start drooling and stuttering. You tillilate a man by leaning way over the desk with your blouse half open as you are asking him if he would like another copy of a report. You might work for the most intelligent men in the world, but because of the way you're dressed, they can't string together a complete sentence.

Ladies, there is nothing wrong with being beautiful. Praise God for your beauty. But do not use your beauty to manipulate a man. Put some clothes on. Have some respect for yourself. Make a man respect you because you deserve respect. Make him respect you because you respect yourself. Make him respect you because you're a child of God, not because of how seductively you're dressed. If that's all a man is paying attention to, he's not respecting you, he's lusting after you.

You've got to let a man know that there are some games you don't play. There are some e-mails you don't wish to see. There are some touches that are inappropriate. Tell him, "Don't send me those kinds of e-mails. Don't massage my shoulders." You've got to let a man know that you only go so far. As a matter of fact, you've got to look at your boss and say, "If you even think that, I'll throw you out the thirty-ninth-floor window and I'll be in jail just as happy as I need to be, because I'm not that kind of person, and you're not going to treat me like that."

Ladies, don't talk to me about sexual harassment. You

have got to draw the line. You have got to tell men, "I don't listen to those types of jokes. You don't touch me in that kind of way. As a matter of fact, I'd rather be in a basement mopping a floor than to be up with you here in the penthouse doing that."

Your looks and your figure are a gift from God. They are nothing you can boast about. You want to be known for your integrity, for your character, for your decency. You don't want to walk around and think that the only way you can get what you want is to manipulate a man. You don't have to do that to get what you want. Instead, think about how to get what you want. *Figure out* how to get what you want. *Pray* for what you want. Don't p-r-e-y on what you want. P-r-a-y for what you want! Get down on your knees and ask the heavenly Father to touch your heart so that you are open to the kind of man He will bring into your life.

5. Bad girls sleep with somebody else's man. John 4:4–30, 39–42 tells the story of Jesus and the Samaritan woman. In John 4:16–18 it is written, "Jesus saith unto her, Go, call thy husband, and come hither. The woman answered and said, I have no husband. Jesus said unto her, Thou hast well said, I have no husband: for thou hast had five husbands; and he whom thou now hast is not thy husband: in that saidst thou truly."

Jesus said something very interesting to the woman: "You have well said that you don't have a husband." But then he added, "The one that you've got now ain't your husband," implying, "The man you're sleeping with now is somebody else's man." Jesus said, "I am not saying he's not somebody's husband. I am saying he isn't your husband."

There are some women who only date married men. There are some women who won't even get attracted to a guy unless they know that guy is married. Some women only date a man they can send home at the end of the day because they are only looking for is sex and/or money.

Ladies, get your own man.

If God is all that we say He is, if God can do all that we say He can do, you don't have to rent a man, you don't have to borrow a man, you don't have to share a man. The reason men get away with all the stuff they get away with is because women are going around acting the way they are acting.

Women have heard the statistics. They are sitting around talking about, "There's only one man for every six women, so I know that I'd better . . ." No! you'd better wait for *your* man. While you're in love with somebody else's man, you're delaying the arrival of your own. God has your man, but the reason He can't send him is because your emotions are all wrapped up with someone else's guy. Let that man alone so you can get who God has for you.

It kills me when I hear ladies say, "But I love him, and he really loves me. You don't understand his situation. He's there with her, but he really doesn't love her. He's just got to be there for the children." Well, then, tell him to give you his home phone number. Tell that man, "Take me by there, 'cause it ought not to bother you if your wife knows about us, because you really don't love her in the first place."

"He's just there," you might say. Yeah, but the fact remains that he *is* there. "There" means he's not "here" where you are. So "he's just there" means that you shouldn't put any emotion into him or be in a relationship with him because you're getting ready to get your feelings hurt, and you're getting ready to get your heart broken.

Women who sleep with married men will believe all kinds of stories. "He ain't sleeping with his wife. He sleeps downstairs. His wife sleeps upstairs. They ain't slept together in three years."

Women will fall for some of the most amazing things, and y'all who date married men are some of the most gullible people on earth. That's why it bothers you when his wife becomes pregnant. "I don't know how I started going with him. I don't know how I fell in love with a married man. We were just talking and we were just friends, and I don't know how it happened."

You know how it happened. Your last boyfriend was a married man. It is a pattern for you. You fall in love with married men. That's what bad girls do. And you hate to break the pattern because you think it's safe. Well, it's not safe. You're the one who's by yourself at Thanksgiving. You're the one who's alone at Christmas. You're the one celebrating your birthday with just you and a cake. You're the one sitting there waiting for someone to run by to have sex. And then, when he finally arrives, he's giving you that old tired line, "You know I'd stay longer, but I can't." Why would you continue to put yourself in that situation?

CHANGE YOUR WICKED WAYS

Solomon closes Proverbs 31 by saying, "Favour is deceitful, and beauty is vain: but a woman that feareth the Lord, she shall be praised. Give her of the fruit of her hands; and let her own works praise her in the gates" (vv. 30–31).

Bad girls, charm will fool you, and beauty is like trouble. It don't last. You will not always be able to manipulate men because of the way you look. There is a younger prettier girl about to get off the next elevator or sitting behind you in the next pew. If you get your thrills from manipulating men with your body, you'd better die at thirty because there is an old lady on the way to your house.

"But a woman that feareth the Lord," a woman who honors God, a woman who seeks to please Him, believe it or not, when all the hype is over, *a good girl,* "she shall be praised." A good girl pleases God. The bad girls might be at all the parties, they might be the ones on the back of the motorcycle; they might be sticking their heads out of the sunroof tops, but the good girls make it to the altar.

After a man uses up the bad girls, sleeps with the easy girls, he marries the one who said no. He marries the one who had some dignity, he marries the one who had some character, he marries the one who had some stuff she wouldn't do, because that's the one he's going to trust when he's gone away on business. That's the one who is going to have his babies. That's the one who is going to raise his children.

So the next time someone asks, "Who can find a virtuous woman?" I hope the answer is, "You can find her right here. You can find her in the pews of churches across America. You can find her in church on any Wednesday. You can find her in church on any Sunday. You can find her in the choir. You can find her in the audience, but rest assured, a good girl can be found."

Where Do Broken Hearts Go?
Can They Find
Their Way Home?

Where Do Broken Hearts Go? Can They Find Their Way Home?

When all is said and done, most of us want to experience the love of another human being. We've talked about how to find a mate, what not to get in a mate, and what you shouldn't do to try to get a mate. We're going to wrap up our discussion by talking about how a broken heart can be repaired and by exploring the fact that all meaningful relationships begin with you and the heavenly Father.

I am convinced that many of you have experienced a broken heart. And if you have ever had your heart broken, you know there isn't any pain like it. I don't care what kind of trouble you've had; I don't care what kind of trouble you've been in. There's no trouble like heart trouble.

When your heart is broken, it doesn't make any difference *what* kind of food is on the table. You aren't hungry. You don't want to eat. Your heart can wake you up out of a sound sleep and ask, "What are you doing trying to go to sleep knowing how bad I feel?" You don't want to talk to anybody. If it weren't for the rent money you wouldn't even go to work. (Now let me just take a little sidestep to say Rent don't care how you feel; Rent don't care how broke your heart is. Rent is going to send you to work—Rent and that other young lady, Car-note-due.)

Everybody is running around the beach, having a good time, but you feel sad. You could do a remake of the Temptations' classic, "I Wish It Would Rain." You want the sunshine and blue skies to please go away. You wish it would rain because raindrops would hide your teardrops. Since you are miserable, you want everyone else to be miserable.

Webster's New Universal Unabridged Dictionary describes the heart as "a hollow muscular organ which by rhythmic contractions and relaxations keeps the blood in circulation throughout the body." That's what it says the heart is. However, when your heart is broken, you can't cut your chest open and see a crack down the middle of the organ that pumps blood from your arteries to your veins. Yet you know it's broken.

When the Bible talks about the heart, the Bible is talking about another definition for the word *heart,* the heart as the center or source of emotions, specifically one's innermost thoughts and feelings. Therefore—pay attention now, don't miss it—when your heart is broken, it means that your emotions have been dealt a devastating blow. The way they say it on the street is, "somebody done messed over the way you feel."

Do you know that there are more songs recorded about people with broken hearts than perhaps any other topic? The only rival might be songs about falling in love. I think there is a reason for that. First, you sing about falling in love, and then a few weeks later you sing about a broken heart. The blues are birthed out of life's painful experiences. I remember a song that said, in essence, to the DJ, "Since we are all miserable here tonight, why don't you play another somebody-done-somebody-wrong song?" Since that seems to be the order of the night, we'll listen to it over and over. Just play another somebody-done-somebody-wrong song.

Now the person who usually teaches you the most about a broken heart is the first person who broke your heart. You go into the relationship thinking that this person will never let you down. You think that this feeling you have—this bliss, this magic, this love—will never end. You enter that first relationship so much in love and you believe that the other person loves you as much as you love him. Why you just know that if you start crying he will catch your tears before they hit the ground. That's some kind of love!

But then the day comes when he says, "Yeah, I love you, but I love you like a sister." And you say, "You didn't love me like no sister when you were hugging me. You didn't love me like no sister when you were kissing me. Now all of a sudden you love me, but you love me like a sister. Well, I don't love you like no brother."

Or he says, "I really like you, but—"

That's the classic one. It just knocks your socks off. Your emotions are in an uproar. You're devastated. You try to stay calm and keep your composure, but you feel like fainting. The only reason you don't just fall out is because you're trying to pretend it doesn't hurt you.

"Yeah, I really like you, but . . . I think we should see other people."

You try everything you can, after you've done *all* you can; you just stand, but you're just wobbling 'cause you know what that means. It means your exclusive relationship is no more. It means, "I'm about to see somebody else other than you."

And so that first relationship ends and you are heartbroken. But it teaches you some lessons that you will never forget. When you get over the hurt, when you come through the pain, you make a promise to God and the world. You (and anyone else who will listen) promise that you aren't *ever* going to let *anybody* hurt you like that anymore. That relationship teaches you how to hold in a certain part of yourself and not to give that part to anybody.

GOD'S PROTECTION AGAINST HEART TROUBLE

God wants to save us from this trouble. So He has established rules that will protect our hearts. In the book of Deuteronomy, the Israelites are about to possess the land of Canaan and Moses is close to the end of his life. He is summarizing what the Israelites have been through on their journey from Egypt, and he is repeating the Law God has given to the people. Then, in the midst of all this law and all this history, Moses says:

Here, O Israel: The Lord our God is one Lord: And thou shalt love the Lord thy God with all thine heart, and with all thy soul, and with all thy might. (Deuteronomy 6:4–5)

God is saying, "Put God first." He would have us know that there is a certain portion of your emotions that must be reserved and put into the bank for God. You can't give them to *anybody* but God because God is the *only* one who can keep them without hurting you. God is saying to us that our love for Him will result in our having a right relationship with Him; and if we have a right relationship with Him, He can keep us from a lot of pain.

So how does a heart get broken? Don't miss this! A heart gets broken when you don't love the Lord with all your heart, and with all your soul, and with all your might. A heart gets broken when you put it in an insecure place. Your emotions get messed over when you put them in an unstable place. A heart gets broken when you put it in a place where it can be broken. Where you put your heart will determine whether or not your heart is going to be broken.

If you have placed your heart in anything that is less
than perfect,

if you have given your emotions over to anything that
is other than flawless,

if you have given your feelings over to anything that
is less than 100 percent guaranteed,

then *know for sure* that your heart has been placed in
a position where you might be the next guest to
check into Heartbreak Hotel.

God wants to teach us how not to give the core of our
emotions to *anybody* but Him. Why you might ask? I'll be
happy to explain. The core of your emotions is the part
of you that can be hurt, crushed, and devastated. God
wants us to learn not to give that part of our heart to anybody but Him.

There is blessing in following God's commands:

Now these are the commandments, the statutes, and
the judgments, which the Lord your God commanded
to teach you, that ye might do them in the land whither ye go to possess it: that thou mightest fear the Lord
thy God, to keep all his statutes and his commandments which I command thee, thou, and thy son, and
thy son's sons, all the days of thy life; and that thy days
may be prolonged. Hear therefore, O Israel, and ob-
serve to do it; that it may be *well with thee,* and that ye
may *increase mightily,* as the Lord God of thy fathers

hath promised thee, in the land that floweth with milk and honey. (Deuteronomy 6:1–3, italics added)

God wants to teach His people how to have a long life. God wants to teach His people how to have a good and productive life. God wants to teach His people how they and their children can have a happy life void of heartbreak. Therefore, God gives us a formula for a good life.

Now don't miss this. A good life, a happy life, a life void of pain depends upon where you put your heart. Therefore, the key verse is found in Deuteronomy 6:5: "Thou shalt love the Lord thy God with all thine heart, and with all thy soul, and with all thy might."

So where do broken hearts go? Can they find their way home? Yes, they can. Deuteronomy 6:5 tells us how, and it tells us where home is. Broken hearts need that because you can't go back home unless you know where home is. And the only place we can totally put our hearts and our emotions and be safe is in *Him*.

OBJECTIONS AND A RESPONSE

"Uh-huh, Preacher, you don't understand; uh-huh, not *my* husband. My husband would *never* do so and so." Listen, you don't know what your husband would do.

"Uh-huh, Preacher, not my wife; she would never—" Listen, you don't *know* what your wife would do.

"Uh-huh, Preacher, you don't understand; not my

momma. My momma would never—" Listen, you don't *know* what your momma would do.

"Uh-huh, Preacher, not my daddy—" Listen, you don't *know* what your daddy would do.

"Uh-huh, Preacher, not my child—" Many parents come up to us at our Christian school, and you know, *their* children never do anything wrong; you know, "Uh-huh, that don't sound like my child—" Listen, you don't *know* what kind of monster he is when you're not around.

"Uh-huh, not my pastor. My pastor would never—" Listen, you don't *know* what your pastor would do.

"Uh-huh, no, not me—"

Listen, you don't *know* what you would do. You can *never* say never. Half the stuff we said we weren't ever going to do, we've already done, and we've got the other half left.

Those of you who are into computers, I'll tell you what Deuteronomy 6:5 does. It gives us the home page —the Web site—of your heart. It tells you the address where your heart should be. It should be at www.welove-God. God said that everybody's heart should be dedicated to Him above all else.

Now God does not mind us loving other stuff. God just doesn't want us to love anything above Him. That's why the first commandment God gave the children of Israel wasn't "Don't steal." That's why it wasn't "Don't kill." That's why it wasn't "Don't commit adultery." That's why it wasn't "Don't bear false witness." The first commandment God gave them was "Don't have thing else above

Me. Don't love anybody or anything more than you love Me. Don't put anybody else in My spot. 'Cause if you put somebody else in My spot, we are going to have some problems."

That's why Jesus said, "Seek ye first the kingdom of God, and his righteousness" (Matthew 6:33), for "no man can serve two masters" (v. 24). You can't be devoted to two things at the same time. You are going to love one of them more than you love the other, and if the other one is God and God finds out that you love somebody more than you love Him, you are going to have trouble. God is the Master, and we are the servants. God is the Creator, and we are the creation. The servant is supposed to be totally dedicated to the Master. The creation is supposed to be totally dedicated to the Creator. Whenever that order is violated, whenever God is here and other stuff is there, whenever you put God under the other stuff, get ready now, 'cause you are going to check into your room at Heartbreak Hotel.

GOD'S PROTECTION FOR OUR CHILDREN

Moses told the Israelites to teach His commands to their children:

These words, which I command thee this day, shall be in thine heart: and thou shalt teach them diligently unto thy children, and shalt talk of them when you sittest in thine house, and when thou walkest by the

way, and when thou liest down, and when thou ris-
est up. (Deuteronomy 6:6–7)

When my daughters Jamie, Janet, and Jasmine reached
twelve years of age, I had a ring ceremony for them. I
bought a ring for each of them. I told them I was giving
them a ring because I loved them, and that the only ring
that could replace the ring I gave them would be an en-
gagement ring. This ring that I gave them was to remind
them of my love for them and to remind them of the rules
they had to obey.

What I was saying to my girls was, "Right now, you
are Daddy's girl. And what I want you to do is give Daddy
your heart. Now I know that the time will come when
a beau is going to come along, and that person is going
to replace me and my ring. But, for now, what I'm saying to my babies is, 'Let Daddy keep your heart.' Why?
'Because Daddy can safeguard your heart.'

"Now, in order for Daddy to guard your heart, Daddy's
girls are going to have to follow Daddy's rules. But when
you follow my rules, you get all of the benefits of Daddy's
house. You get food, you get to wear clothes that Daddy
buys, you get private school and Daddy's paying the tuition,
you get to go to the beauty shop every two weeks, you
get to have everything that you need. But if I'm going to
safeguard your heart, and if you are going to enjoy these
benefits, you've got to follow some rules.

"Number one, no dating until you are sixteen years old."
I personally don't understand parents who let seventh and

eighth graders—eleven- and twelve-year-old girls— run around talking about, "I got a boyfriend." Come on. There ain't a boyfriend; they don't know anything about a boyfriend. What do they know about a boyfriend? What are you going to do with a boyfriend at eleven?

Let me reiterate. These are the rules for my house. Now you say, "Why, pastor, you are just too hard, and if I was you I'd . . ." Well, you do what you're going to do at your house and I'll do what I'm going to do at my house. But I told my girls, "No dating until you are sixteen."

I told my girls, "No phone calls from boys until you are in high school." What you got to talk to somebody about when you're nine? What you got to talk about when you're eleven? You ain't got *nothing* to talk to no boy about. I told my girls, "No being alone with a boy *ever*. You have no business being alone with a boy. Don't worry, if you need to go somewhere, I've got plenty of guys available. Preachers. Deacons. Security guard. Somebody will get you where you need to go."

I told my girls, "You cannot receive gifts, letters, or cards from anybody without discussing it with your mother or me." Let me come into one of my girls' rooms and find some gift, card, or letter, and they talk about some boy gave it—"You ain't got no business receiving anything from a boy and you ain't told me about it. What's he giving you something for? What could he possibly give you that I can't give you?"

I told my girls, "No working with boys on school projects. There are some girls in your class; you ain't got to work with any boy on a project. There are some girls in your class you-all can work with."

I'm going to say it one more time. If you think I'm too strict, you run your house the way you want to and I will run my house the way I want to. *But be careful.* Because whenever a father does not have rules for his girls (and boys), he is setting his children up for disaster. You are the father. Society is not supposed to tell you how to run your house. The folks next door are not supposed to tell you how to run your house. The people down the street are not supposed to tell you how to run your house. *You* are supposed to run your house according to your relationship with God and your knowledge of the Bible. That's how you run your house.

Now I didn't establish these rules because I didn't love Jamie, Janet, and Jasmine. I didn't establish these rules because I wanted to stifle their growth. I didn't establish these rules because I didn't trust them. I trust all of them. I established these rules because I asked my daughters for their hearts. And since they gave me their hearts, I've got to safeguard them and keep them from being broken. I know that there are some things that can break their hearts that they are not aware of.

WHEN WE DON'T FOLLOW OUR HEAVENLY FATHER'S RULES

The principles that apply in my daughters' lives apply to the world in general. God says, "You want to be happy? You want to live a long life? You want to increase mightily? You want to live in My house? You want to enjoy My benefits? Then give Me your heart. Love Me with all your heart and with all your soul and with all your might. If you do this, I can protect you. If you do this, I can make you certain promises. But when you give Me your heart, there's one thing I need you to do to help Me keep your heart from being broken. I need you to obey My rules. That means that whatever I say to you, I need you to *do* it. Because the things I say to you will keep you from having your heart broken."

If we are honest, we would admit that 90 percent of all of our heartbreaks come from the fact that we've done something we didn't get Daddy's permission to do. And we followed that little voice that said "Go ahead. It's no big deal." So I say that most of our troubles come from the fact that we do stuff we don't have Daddy's permission to do. In fact, most of our heartbreaks come about because we have directly violated one or more of God's rules.

Can I go there? You knew that person was married when you went out with him. He gave you his office number and his pager number, but he wouldn't give you his home number. That's because there was someone there that he didn't want to know about you. You knew that then. That was a heartbreak you didn't have to have.

You knew that that person wasn't saved when you gave him your phone number. Sure, he was good looking and had nice manners. He took you to some nice places. But everytime you asked him to go to church with you, he had something else to do. Or, he came, but he looked at his watch the whole time wondering when it was going to be over. Or, he said that he believed in God, but all that "church stuff" wasn't necessary. Now you're in love with him and you're torn up because you know what the Word says about being unequally yoked. That is a heartbreak you didn't have to have.

You knew that you could get pregnant when you had sex with him. You're not crazy. You know how babies are made. But the first problem was not you-all having sex; the first problem was your being alone together. Anybody knows that if you rub two sticks together long enough, they are bound to get hot and you're going to have a fire. You knew that when you started. That is a heartbreak you didn't have to have.

You knew when you took that money from your job that it wasn't your money. You knew that you could lose your job. Likewise, you knew you could get hooked on that stuff when you first started smoking it. You knew it then. Also, you knew when you first sniffed it off the glass that it could hook you. God says, "Give Me your heart, obey My rules, and I'll protect you."

While I'm on this subject, brothers, why do you think that God chose circumcision as the sign of His covenant with man? (You *do* know that that's a sign that God chose to show a man that we have a relationship, don't you?) There are two reasons. Number one, because a man has to handle that object several times a day. And every time he handles it, it's supposed to remind him of his relationship with God. And number two, if there's any part of his body that's apt to get him into trouble, that's the part. And so God said, "Every time you touch it I want you to be reminded of the fact that you have a relationship with Me. I'm not going to give you a ring like Reverend Meeks gave Jamie, Janet, and Jasmine, 'cause you might lose that. *This* is what I'll give you." Whack! Whack! Whack! You can't lose that. (Pardon me for being graphic. I'm just trying to keep it real.)

So most of our heartbreaks and most of our heartaches come from the fact that we don't obey Daddy's rules. And when we disobey Daddy's rules, we are candidates for a broken heart. That's why Jesus never had a broken heart. Because I heard Him say, "I do always those things that please my Father" (see John 8:29). He became disappointed, but He never had a broken heart. He never had to say, "Well, Preacher, get me out of this mess."

When a heart is broken it has been removed from the home. When a heart is broken it has lost its way home. When a heart is broken—pay attention to this now—it has either violated a rule or it has loved somebody or sought after something with more might than it sought after God. Are you with me? Somebody is saying, "Wait a minute, Preacher. I thought I was marrying a good Christian man. I thought I was in the will of God, and that person still hurt me."

I say, again, whenever we allow out hearts to love somebody and seek after something with more might than we love and seek after God, that something is going to break our hearts. You see, when you start dating a person, you talk to that person forever. Ain't no mountain high enough, ain't no valley low enough, ain't no river wide enough to keep you from getting to that person. You talk on the phone all the time. You go to lunch, you go to dinner, you spend all kinds of time together, but during that same period of time in your life you don't have enough time for God. Am I right about it? You ain't even enough time to get up and say "Good morning" to God 'cause you're on your way to the telephone. You don't pray, you don't read the Scriptures, you don't go to church, you don't spend time thinking about or talking to God, you don't witness, you don't share your faith. It's just hard to convince God that this person who gets all of your time, affection, and attention doesn't mean as much or more to you than He does. Am I right about that?

And it's not just another *person*. God doesn't even want you to love your *job* more than you love Him. God doesn't want you to love your *children* more than you love Him. God doesn't want you to love your *husband* or your *wife* more than you love Him. God doesn't want *anybody* or *anything* to be in His spot.

And so I close by telling you that God will not let anything we place above Him to give us pleasure. God will not let anything we place above Him give us peace. I don't care what it is. God won't let your education, your family, your boyfriend, or your dog bring you joy if you place it above Him.

BRINGING OUR HEARTS HOME

"Well, Preacher, my heart is broken. I messed up. All that stuff that you said is right. But I still need to know, Can my heart get back home?

"Oh, Preacher, I messed up, but I want to know, Can my heart can get back to God?"

Yes, it can. Your heart can find its way back home. And here's how: You need to make a conscious decision to take your heart away from your career or from that person who is so much on your mind or from that thing that interests you so much and *let it go back to where it belongs.*

Yes, broken hearts can go back home. Broken hearts can be healed when they are yielded to the One who will never break them. Let me hear you say, "Situation, you know what you are. Give me my heart back. Because my heart is going back to God."

This day your heart can go back home. Your heart can go back to where it belongs. Your heart can be put back into the right position, the position where you can say, "I love the lord with all my heart and all my soul and all my might."

You know the story of the Prodigal Son (Luke 15:11–32). The boy left home. He took his heart away from his father's house. He got so low there was no sunshine in his life. But one day he came to a conscious decision and said, "I will arise and go to my father."

And listen to what he said then: "Maybe my daddy

will accept me back home. Maybe my daddy will find a place for me back home."

You need to decide that you going to take your heart and go back home. You've got to stop hanging your heart out there, letting people mess it over. You've got to stop hanging your heart out there, letting people walk all over it. You've got to stop hanging your heart out there, putting it in a place where it can be hurt. Get up *now*. Go back home. Get up *this day* and decide, "I will go back home."

When the Prodigal Son started walking, the Bible says his father saw him "a great way off" and said, "That's my boy." Somebody said, "But he's dirty." But the daddy said, "That's my boy." Somebody said, "But he's raggedy." But the father said, "That's my boy." Somebody said, "But he's smelly." But the father said, "That's my boy." Somebody said, "But he left home." But the father said, "That's my boy. And I'm going to accept him with open arms."

I came to encourage someone today that you *can* get up; you *can* take your heart back home.

Now the devil will be standing there saying, "But, God, she fell in love with a married man." But God will say, "That's my child." Somebody will say, "But, God, he fell in love with an unbeliever." But God will say, "That's my child." Somebody will say, "But he put that job before you." But God will say, "That's my child."

All you've got to do is get up. All you have to do is *turn around*. All you have to do is say, "I'm going back to God. Ain't letting no man walk over me no more. I'm going back to God. Ain't letting no woman walk over me tonight. I'm going back to God. Daddy, here's my heart. Father, here's my heart. Keep my heart; protect my heart. I want You above everybody else. I want You before I love anybody else.

"Father, here are my tears, here are my emotions, here is my love. If I'm going to love anybody, I'm going to love You. If I'm ever going to cry over anybody, I'm going to cry about You. If I'm ever going to think about anybody all day long, I'm going to think about You.

"God, I come to You this day in the only way I know how. If I've walked away from You, I'm sorry. If I've given my heart to somebody else, I'm sorry. Today I turn to *You*. Take my heart, take my mind, take my emotions, and *let me be Your child*. And now, I accept the fact that You have forgiven me and have cleansed me and I'm Your daughter and I'm Your son. Thank you, Daddy, for letting me come back home."

Why don't you call two friends and let them know that you have come back to God. They will rejoice with you because now they will know that your heart is safe back home with the Father.

★ ★ ★

Eternal God, our Father, we thank You for the privilege of prayer. We know that You hear and answer prayer. We thank You so much for the privilege of sharing Your Word. We need You to be our Teacher; we need You to be our Preacher. Somebody's heart is broken, and he doesn't know how to get back to You. And so,

God, we pray that You would teach us and preach to us. If there are people who are reading this who don't know You, heavenly Father, Holy Spirit have them to know that all they have to do is say, "Jesus, come into my heart." And so, God, receive all of the glory and all of the praise. In Jesus' name. Amen.

For Further Study

The material in this book was originally presented as a series of sermons at Salem Baptist Church, 11800 S. Indiana, Chicago, Illinois 60628. An audiotape series of those sermons is available from Media Ministry, P.O. Box 288867, Chicago, Illinois, 60628, 1-866-586-3300 under the title *Life Changing Relationships* and *Where Do Broken Hearts Go?* by the Reverend James T. Meeks (Chicago: SBC Ministries, 2001).

Boteach, Shmuley. *Dating Secrets of the Ten Commandments.* New York: Doubleday, 2000.

Clark, Jeramy. *I Gave Dating a Chance: A Biblical Perspective to Balance the Extremes.* Colorado Springs: Water-Brook, 2000.

Cloud, Henry, and John Townsend. *Boundaries in Dating.* Grand Rapids: Zondervan, 2000.

Gaddis, Patricia Riddle. *Dangerous Dating: Helping Young Women Say No to Abusive Relationships.* Colorado Springs: Harold Shaw, 2000.

Hammond, Michelle McKinney. *Get a Love Life.* Eugene, Ore.: Harvest House, 2000.

_____. *If Men Are Like Buses Then How Do I Catch One.* Sisters, Ore.: Multnomah, 2000.

Harris, Joshua. *I Kissed Dating Goodbye: A New Attitude Toward Relationships and Romance.* Sisters, Ore.: Multnomah, 1997.

Harris, Joshua, with Shannon Harris and Nicole Mahaney. *I Kissed Dating Goodbye: The Study Guide.* Sisters, Ore.: Multnomah, 1999.

Jackson, Chris. *The Black Christian Singles Guide to Dating and Sexuality.* Grand Rapids: Zondervan, 1999.

Warren, Neil Clark. *Two Dates or Less: How to Know if Someone Is Worth Pursuing in Two Dates or Less.* Nashville: Thomas Nelson, 1999.

Young, Ben, and Samuel Adams. *10 Commandments of Dating.* Nashville: Thomas Nelson, 1999.

The original sermons that inspired the writing of this book are available by contacting:

Media Ministry
Salem Baptist Church of Chicago
P.O. Box 288867
Chicago, Illinois 60628
toll free 866-586-3300

Tape 1 Who Let the Dogs Out?
Tape 2 Watch Out for Bad Girls
Tape 3 How to Find a Mate

Available in Audio, Video, or CD

In addition, you can also obtain a catalog of Pastor Meeks' most popular messages upon request.

Moody Press, a ministry of Moody Bible Institute,
is designed for education, evangelization, and edification.
If we may assist you in knowing more about Christ
and the Christian life, please write us without obligation:
Moody Press, c/o MLM, Chicago, Illinois 60610.